STONE AGE BOY

SATOSHI KITAMURA

WOLVERINE

WILD BOAR

ROE DEER

AUK

The author and publisher would like to thank Alison Roberts
of the Ashmolean Museum, Oxford, for her invaluable help in the making of this book.

First published 2007 by Walker Books Ltd
87 Vauxhall Walk, London SE11 5HJ

2 4 6 8 10 9 7 5 3 1

© 2007 Satoshi Kitamura

The right of Satoshi Kitamura to be identified as author/illustrator of this work
has been asserted by him in accordance with the Copyright, Designs and Patents Act 1988

This book has been typeset in Century Old Style

Printed in Singapore

British Library Cataloguing in Publication Data:
a catalogue record for this book is available from the British Library

ISBN: 978-1-4063-0335-3

www.walkerbooks. co.uk

WALKER BOOKS
AND SUBSIDIARIES
LONDON • BOSTON • SYDNEY • AUCKLAND

An amazing thing once happened to me.

I was wandering in the woods

when I tripped and found myself

falling down

down

down.

7

When I woke up, I was in a cold, dark place.

I could see daylight in the distance and I stumbled towards it.

Outside, everything was different.

I realized I was lost. Completely lost.

So I walked and walked

and walked…

Then, to my relief, I saw someone – a girl.

She was about my age, but she didn't look like any of the girls I knew.

And I don't think I looked like any of the boys she knew.

11

She took me home to meet her family – and what a family it was!

They looked very strange, but they were kind to me and gave me some stew.

I couldn't understand anything they were saying,

though I worked out my new friend's name was Om.

Then I must have fallen asleep.

The next morning, Om showed me round the camp.

Everyone seemed busy and had a job to do.

Over the next few days I saw so much I'd never seen before.

Om's people had no knives and forks, no plastic, no metal even.

Everything they had was made of wood, stone, animal skins or bones.

I saw them...

MAKING FIRE

By striking flint stones together or turning a wooden drill. Fire is used for cooking, to keep warm and sometimes to scare animals.

MAKING TOOLS

By flint knapping.

The flints are chipped, trimmed and sharpened, and then made into knives, spearheads and scrapers for cleaning animal skins.

I had a go, but it was very difficult.

USING TOOLS

Cutting a slice out of a bone

Sharpening it on a grindstone

Piercing a hole

It's a sewing needle!

Ornaments

Tools are used to make wood, antlers and bones into bowls, spears and ornaments.

16

Using a throwing stick you can throw a spear faster and further.

PREPARING & USING
ANIMAL SKINS

Scraping the
hide clean

Cutting it

Piercing holes

Drying it

Sewing it together.

Skinning
a deer

Using skins
to repair
a tent

PREPARING & COOKING FOOD

Smoking
meat

Cutting
meat

Drying
meat

Drying
fish

Boiling soup
by putting
a red-hot
stone into
a leather bag

Grilling
meat

One afternoon we went to the river.

The little ones picked berries and nuts, but Om and I watched the men fishing.

They held their pointed spears high and stood as still as trees.

Then, suddenly, *swoosh!* their spears dropped down like lightning

and came up again spiking wriggling silver fish.

Suddenly a boy ran up, shouting and pointing to the hills. At once several people grabbed their spears and followed him. Om and I followed them.

Slowly, slowly, we crept forwards until we saw – a reindeer!
It was standing alone, munching the grass.

At a signal, the others ran towards it, yelling and throwing their spears.

Om and I didn't have spears, but we yelled anyway. It was so exciting!

A spear caught the reindeer in its side, and it fell to the ground.

That night we had a party to celebrate.

We cooked the reindeer over a great fire and there was music and dancing.

I joined in on air guitar.

As the days became weeks, Om and her people

taught me many things. I was very happy.

Then one day Om took me to a special place.

We walked a long way until we came to the mouth of a cave.

Om struck flint stones together to make fire. She lit a torch and we went in.

Wow!

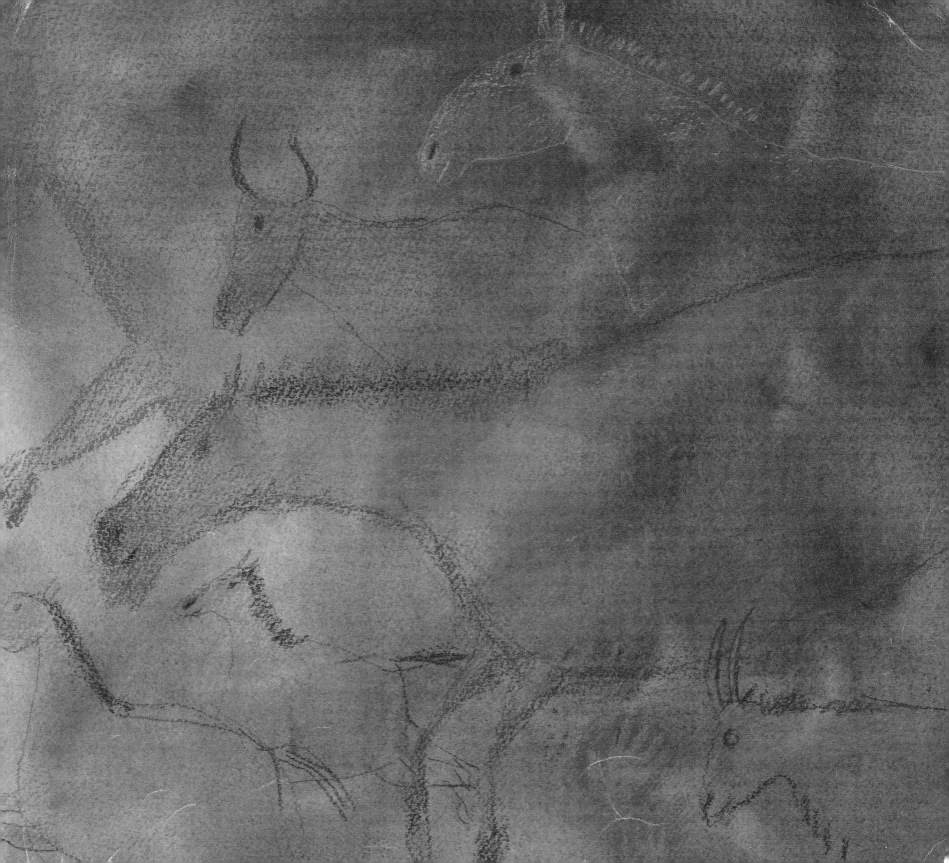

It took me a moment to realize the animals were only paintings.

In the flickering light of the torch they looked real,

as if they were running all around us.

Om went over to the tools and paints the artists had left and began to draw.

Suddenly, I saw something move in the darkness.

It was a bear, a big furious cave bear!

I shouted at Om to run

and turned to face the bear with my spear.

I felt very small.

Suddenly the ground gave way …

and I found myself

falling down

down

down.

When I woke up the bear had gone.

So had Om.

I rushed outside.

The air felt ... different. Warmer.

I walked a long way, calling for Om. But I never found her.

Instead I found I was back home.

When I told my family what had happened, they didn't believe me.

They said I'd only been gone a few hours

and I must have fallen asleep and dreamt it.

Years passed, but I never forgot my friend Om.

I am an archaeologist now (that's me in the glasses).

Everywhere I go, I look in the past for signs of Om.

And I never stop learning from her and her people.

Was it a dream? Maybe …

Maybe not.

Index

Stone Age

cave paintings

first
pottery

first
farmers

keeping
animals

first
towns

farmin

15,000 BCE 14,000 BCE 13,000 BCE 12,000 BCE 11,000 BCE 10,000 BCE 9,000 BCE 8,000 BCE 7,000 BC

Author's Note

I've always been interested in cave paintings. I'd seen them in photos and books for years and they fascinated me. So one summer I decided to go to the south of France where many of the caves are and see them for real. It was one of the most memorable experiences of my life. They were painted so beautifully – whoever did them must have drawn a great deal, and the animals must have been very important to them. But what struck me above all was the sheer joy in the work. I could see that the artists were having a great time – the animals looked as though they were running and dancing around in the dark caves. This book is the result of my daydreams about those painters, and all the people of the Stone Age.

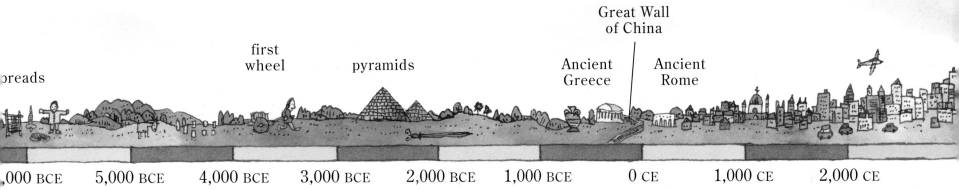

Great Wall of China

first wheel

pyramids

Ancient Greece

Ancient Rome

…reads

,000 BCE   5,000 BCE   4,000 BCE   3,000 BCE   2,000 BCE   1,000 BCE   0 CE   1,000 CE   2,000 CE

WOOLLY RHINOCEROS

ARCTIC
FOX

RED DEER

PINE MARTEN

MOUNTAIN HARE